5 7
P9-CKL-467

HOT

Celebrity Biographies

Shaun White

SNOW AND SKATEBOARD CHAMPION

MARTY GITLIN

Enslow Publishers, Inc.
40 Industrial Road
Box 398
Berkeley Heights, NJ 07922
USA
http://www.enslow.com

Library of Congress Cataloging-in-Publication Data
Gitlin, Marty.
  Shaun White : snow and skateboard champion / Marty Gitlin.
      p. cm. — (Hot celebrity biographies)
  Includes bibliographical references and index.
  Summary: "A biography about Olympic gold medallist snowboarder Shaun White. Find out how he started snowboarding and skateboarding, and what he plans to do in the future"—Provided by publisher.
  ISBN-13: 978-0-7660-3212-5
  ISBN-10: 0-7660-3212-4
  1. White, Shaun, 1986—Juvenile literature. 2. Snowboarders—United States–Biography—Juvenile literature. I. Title.
  GV857.S57W554 2009
  796.939092–dc22
  [B]
                                            2008026465

Paperback ISBN-13: 978-0-7660-3627-7
Paperback ISBN-10: 0-7660-3627-8

Printed in the United States of America

10 9 8 7 6 5 4 3 2 1

Photographs: Nick Laham/Getty Images, 1; Lionel Cironneau/AP Images, 4, 7; Greg Baker/AP Images, 9, 32; Douglas C. Piza/AP Images, 10; LaFonzo Rachal Carter/The San Bernardino Sun/AP Images, 12; Bill Ross/AP Images, 14, 17; Christian Petersen/Getty Images, 21; Kim Johnson Flodin/AP Images, 22; Jerome T. Nakagawa/AP Images, 25; Reed Saxon/AP Images, 26; Jack Dempsey/AP Images, 27, 29; Tim Larsen/AP Images, 31; Chris Carlson/AP Images, 33; Nathan Bilow/AP Images, 35, 40; Garry Jones/AP Images, 36, 39; Ryan Pearson/AP Images, 43

Cover photo: Shaun White rides in the men's skateboard vert competition during the 2004 Summer X Games. Nick Laham/Getty Images.

Contents

Medal of Honor

Shaun White flew through the air with his usual ease and grace. His feet were strapped to his snowboard. He wore a bandanna on his head and a United States team uniform on his chilled body. It was the half-pipe event at the 2006 Winter Olympics in Turin, Italy. All White had to do was land without falling to advance to the next round. But the teenager did something he rarely did. He fell.

White got mad at himself. He didn't train for years to fall down on the biggest stage in the world for winter athletes. He didn't become a champion snowboarder just to ruin a chance at a gold medal in the Winter Olympics. "I was like, 'You have to land this,'" he recalled. "'You *have* to do this. You're at the *Olympics*!'"

He was now in seventh place. Only the top six snowboarders reached the finals. White had one more chance left to make the top six. Thousands of snowboarding fans were watching him. Millions of television viewers around the world were watching him too.

◀ *Shaun White trains on the half-pipe during the 2006 Olympics.*

White realized that if he made one mistake, he was headed back to the United States without a medal. He already had won the Winter X Games for extreme sport athletes. But he knew that critics would say that he couldn't beat the best snowboarders in the world when the pressure was really on. And he prided himself on his ability to rise to the occasion.

Soon he was gliding down the half-pipe and flying through the air again. The song "Back in Black" by the famous rock group AC/DC began playing on the loudspeaker. He stuck one landing, then another. White was on his way to a flawless run when it mattered the most. The judges rewarded him with a score of 45.3 out of 50 possible points. It was the best score of the day for any of the snowboarders.

THE PRESSURE'S ON

Shaun White had made it to the Olympic finals. But he still couldn't celebrate. He could not simply match that performance in the finals. He had to improve on it. After all, he was shooting for the gold medal. And only a near-perfect run would earn him one.

As if the pressure of the finals wasn't enough, White discovered that the dry mountain air had caused his nose to start bleeding. A television crew noticed and rushed toward him. He figured the last thing he needed was the media to

▲ *Shaun White is recognized worldwide for his remarkable skills in snowboarding and skateboarding.*

ruin his concentration. He knew his focus had to be the sharpest it had been since he arrived in Italy. Shaun somehow escaped the cameras. Soon he was back into the half-pipe. He didn't want to think too much. It was time to let his instincts take over. He had gone up and down the half-pipe thousands of times in his life. Many people considered him to be the best in the world. Now it was time to show it.

He couldn't go on a safe run like his last one just to earn enough points to continue. He needed to impress the judges with a difficult routine and a touch of style. And it would have to be perfect. White hit the half-pipe with greater force

WHAT'S IT LIKE TO WIN A GOLD MEDAL?

Shaun White won a gold medal in the 2006 Winter Olympics. But what he had done didn't fully sink in until the next day when he woke up. He opened his eyes and saw the medal next to him in bed.

White spoke about the experience with his family. They reminded him that no matter what happened the rest of his life, it was an achievement that nobody could ever take away from him.

than he did in his earlier runs. He launched himself into the air six times. Every landing was soft and flawless.

White completed a "McTwist," spinning around one-and-a-half times while doing a front flip. He nailed a "Frontside 1080," which meant he had to do three 360-degree spins. That adds up to 1,080 degrees—which is how the move gets its name. White also completed a perfect "Backside 900," landing after two-and-a-half clockwise spins. The fans screamed with delight as he pumped his fist into the air. The judges had awarded him with a 46.8, easily the best of the competition.

BEST OF THE BEST

Now it was time to test his patience. He had to wait while others attempted to beat his score. But none could match his brilliant performance. The last rider had finished his run on the half-pipe. And no one had beaten White's score. White had won the gold medal. He jumped into the arms of his teammates in celebration. Winning the Winter Olympics meant more to White than just earning a first-place medal. He had raised his sport to another level. Snowboarding no longer was just an extreme sport for teenagers. The entire world had seen how much talent and athleticism it required.

The United States flag was raised and "The Star-Spangled Banner" was played during the awards ceremony. White accepted his gold medal with pride. Tears rolled down his cheeks. But it wasn't until later that he fully realized what he had done. "It hits you the next day," he said. "You're like, 'Wow, did that seriously just happen?' I got a gold medal. I guess I'm an athlete now."

▶ *Shaun White celebrates his gold medal at the 2006 Olympic games.*

Heart of a Champion

Shaun White's life got off to a difficult start. When he was born in 1986, he suffered from a heart problem. It affected the supply of oxygen to his heart and lowered the amount of oxygen in his blood. He had to have two surgeries to fix it.

▲ *Shaun White competes in the 2001 World Cup Snowboard competition.*

Roger and Kathy White raised Shaun and his brother Jesse and sister Kerri in Carlsbad, California, a city near San Diego. Shaun's parents were far more protective of him due to the heart problem, even after the operations fixed it. They did promote an active lifestyle, however. Roger and Kathy had athletic backgrounds. Roger had been a water surfer for more than thirty years.

Shaun refused to let his heart problem prevent him from playing sports. Just like his brother and sister, he enjoyed surfing. He also worked on simple skateboarding moves with Jesse in their backyard. He played soccer and jumped on a trampoline. These activities ended up helping him in future skateboarding and snowboarding events.

HITTING THE SLOPES

The most frequent family activity was skiing. The group often drove several hours in the winter to Big Bear Mountain. There, Shaun began to display the fearless attitude he would become known for in his professional career. He was barely aware of his fellow skiers as he swooshed through the snow.

His mother worried about his safety. She remained fearful about Shaun after having almost lost him as an infant. When Shaun was six, she suggested that he switch to snowboarding. She thought snowboarding would be less dangerous to him.

▲ *White started winning snowboarding events at a young age.*

"He was crazy on skis," said Kathy White. "I thought maybe on a snowboard he'll [just sit] and go slow."

The resort didn't provide snowboarding lessons to anyone under twelve years old. So, Roger agreed to take lessons and pass his knowledge on to his son. Shaun also learned from his brother Jesse.

Soon he was ruining his mother's idea that snowboarding would slow him down. He was sliding faster and jumping higher than Jesse could even dream about. In fact, it took Shaun just one day to display snowboarding skills greater than those of his older brother. It quickly became obvious that Shaun was a natural.

CHASING THE DREAM

Roger and Kathy wanted to support Shaun's talent and love for the sport. They also knew that his sister Kerri was showing some impressive ability. So, they entered both Shaun and Kerri in as many snowboarding competitions as possible.

It wasn't easy. Traveling to these events cost money. Roger worked for the water department, and Kathy was a waitress. The Whites were far from wealthy. Other snowboarders stayed at the expensive resorts where the contests took place. The Whites lived out of a thirty-year-old van they nicknamed "Big Mo." The vehicle looked strangely out of place in the parking lot alongside the expensive sports cars and sport utility vehicles owned by those who could afford to stay in the resorts.

Shaun wasted no time showing his parents that it was worth the effort. At age seven, he entered his first snowboarding competition and won! The shocking win earned him a spot in the twelve-and-under division of the United States Amateur Snowboard Association National Championships. Despite being several years younger than most of his opponents, he still finished eleventh.

Encouraged by his success, Shaun continued to compete against snowboarders almost twice his age. He amazed his opponents and snowboarding officials with his ability to

ALL IN THE FAMILY

Shaun White's brother Jesse spent several years managing the Burton Snowboards team that Shaun had joined. Jesse also managed other snowboarders for Burton and even helped Shaun design new clothing and snowboards.

Jesse said there are strong similarities and differences between Shaun and their father, Roger. "I think Shaun got a lot of dad's competitive nature, his drive, and his strength," Jesse said. "It makes me laugh to think about how similar they are. They even walk alike. Seriously, it's really weird."

The father and son do have a few differences, though. "They are different in their ability to assess situations," Jesse continued. "(Dad) is great, but he has definitely made some wrong decisions when on a snowboard. . . . Shaun has this knack of seeing things beforehand, assessing them, and making the right choice."

▲ *Shaun White hangs out with his father, Roger White, at the 2006 Winter X Games.*

explode into jumps far higher than those of the other kids. The extra time in the air also allowed him to show off spins and twists that others couldn't do. His opponents never soared high enough in the air to develop those tricks.

KILLER INSTINCT

Laid-back and friendly in his personal life, Shaun had a killer instinct in competition. That included the simplest board games at home with his friends and family. But it was especially true in snowboarding. Both his talent and his desire to win pushed him to greatness.

Soon the sports world started taking notice. By the time Shaun was nine years old, he was winning every event in his age group. The trophies began piling up in the White home. Word of his talent eventually reached skateboarding legend Tony Hawk, who also enjoys snowboarding. Hawk predicted that Shaun would be the future of the sport. This praise earned him the nickname "Future Boy."

Hawk has called Shaun White "one of the most amazing athletes on the planet." He first saw Shaun snowboard at Big Bear when Shaun was just nine years old. "He was just this little pixie with a giant helmet, coming down the half-pipe. Now, he's grown into his own style—plus he can do tricks five feet higher than everyone else does them."

Shaun hated being known as "Future Boy." He wanted to be recognized for his current achievements. It wasn't easy because he didn't enjoy a pain-free journey to the top. In the few years after he began competing, Shaun broke both his hand and foot and even fractured his skull. But he still won five national championships in the twelve-and-under category in the mid- to late-1990s. There was simply no stopping him.

His family made certain of that. Shaun appreciated his parents' sacrifices. They spent $20,000 a year on travel, food, equipment, and other expenses. Shaun certainly couldn't contribute. No matter how many trophies he won, he earned no prize money as an amateur athlete.

GOING PRO

That was about to change. At age thirteen, he decided to turn professional. This allowed him not only to be eligible for event winnings, but also to earn money by endorsing products. A company called Burton Snowboards realized Shaun's potential and signed him to an endorsement contract. Shaun White had just become a teenager. But he was already on his way to stardom.

Rise of the Flying Tomato

Whatever the competition, White had an intense desire to win. But the smaller the challenge, the less he enjoyed winning. That was the problem for White as an amateur snowboarder. The better he became, the more he distanced

▲ *Shaun White hangs out at his house in Aspen before the 2006 Winter X Games.*

SNOWBOARDING EVENTS

Half-pipe: An event that takes place on a long ramp shaped like a "U"

Slopestyle: An event in which riders compete by doing various jumps

Superpipe: An event in which riders compete on an extended half-pipe

himself from the field. And the easier it became for him to win, the less it meant to him.

Becoming a professional brought the challenge of snowboarding back to White. He could no longer be the best every time. He was now competing against much more experienced snowboarders. In his first year as a professional, he managed several top-ten finishes. But the days of adding to his trophy case every month were over—at least for a while.

White welcomed the demands of matching his skills with older teenagers and adults. He didn't want the other athletes to think of him as just a pesky kid with potential. He wanted to win. And by age fourteen in 2001, he was doing what he did as a young child. He was beating older and more experienced snowboarders. "I wanted to be recognized more for my riding talent than my age," White said in early 2002. "I wanted to make that step from being the cute little kid to being associated with the older riders."

THE FLYING TOMATO

The Winter X Games feature extreme sports such as snowboarding. Extreme sports are fast-paced sports outside the mainstream. The snowboarding event became popular around the same time White was rising to the top of his sport.

It was no coincidence. A growing number of fans found the red-haired kid fascinating. They had reason to—and not just because he was a fourteen-year-old kid competing against adults. By that year, White already had become one of the best snowboarders in the United States. He placed seventh in the slopestyle and ninth in the superpipe competitions in the 2001 Winter X Games. Instead of being known as "Future Kid," he earned the nickname "The Flying Tomato" for his red hair and ability to soar through the air.

Some people thought White would qualify for the 2002 U.S. Winter Olympic team because of his early success. The Olympics were going to take place in Salt Lake City, Utah, which was just a short distance from White's California home. Even the media paid attention to White. *Sports Illustrated for Kids* magazine featured White on its Winter Olympics Preview issue. Fans were saying he might win a gold medal, despite his young age. White didn't even make the team. He missed the cut by a third of a point and was forced to watch the competition on TV. He did finish second in both the slopestyle and superpipe events at the 2002

SHAUN'S MUSICAL TASTES

Shaun White loves rock music from earlier generations. His favorite group is Led Zeppelin. Led Zeppelin reached its peak in the mid-1970s, more than ten years before White was born. But White has pictures of the group on the walls of his California home.

White even titled his snowboarding DVD *The White Album*. That's the same name as one of the most famous albums by The Beatles. The Beatles are considered by many to be the greatest band of all time. They were performing more than twenty years before White was born.

Winter X Games. But he would have to wait for a chance to try again at the 2006 Winter Olympics.

ADDING ANOTHER SPORT

He was not an Olympian yet, but soon he would be the only two-sport star in the world of extreme sports. White focused on skateboarding during the summer of 2002. Though already skilled at that sport, he learned more tricks of the trade from Tony Hawk and other top skateboarders. He joined Hawk's Gigantic Skateboard Tour and prepared to compete professionally in 2003.

But snowboarding was still White's focus. He was disappointed not to make the 2002 Winter Olympic team. This drove him to become the best snowboarder in the world.

And his dedication paid off in 2003 when he won almost every event on the schedule. White earned the gold medal in both the slopestyle and superpipe events at the Winter X Games. That year, he was named the Best Action Sports Athlete in the X Games.

White's success resulted in a ton of publicity. In August 2003, an 80-foot-tall image of White was placed on two sides of a tower in Los Angeles to promote the Summer X Games, his first as a skateboarder. He was also featured as a character on a video snowboarding game.

"A guy like Shaun comes along once every 10 years," said Gus Buckner, who works in the marketing industry. "Shaun is going to be the next icon of extreme sports."

▶ *White now excels in both snowboarding and skateboarding.*

A Star Is Born

The overwhelming success of the 2003 snowboarding season didn't prevent White from also throwing himself into professional skateboarding. In fact, the idea of being a two-sport star became more exciting to him than ever. White didn't wait long. Just three weeks after completing his 2003 snowboarding season, he competed in the Slam City Jam North American Skateboarding Championships in Canada. The result was a fourth-place performance in the vert competition. The vert is a skateboarding event that is held on a U-shaped vertical ramp. It was a strong finish considering his lack of experience.

During his early skateboarding events, White confirmed what he had suspected all along. The time he spent as a snowboarder helped him immensely in the skateboarding world. He had the ability to leap higher, create better twists in the air, and land more firmly than his opponents in both sports. All he needed was consistency. White's fourth-place finish in Canada earned him a spot in both the Gravity

◀ *Shaun White—also known as "The Flying Tomato"—arrives at the 2007 ESPY Awards.*

Games and the Summer X Games. Though he was not shocked at his success, others marveled at his easy transition from snowboarding to skateboarding.

Cody Dresser is associate editor of *Transworld Snowboarding* and a former pro rider. He said that many pro snowboarders dream of being a pro skateboarder as well. "No one's done it. It's bad enough that Shaun White destroys everyone whenever he enters a snow contest, but now he's a pro vert skater and living out every rider's dream. How sick is that?"

SERIOUS SKILLS

White was just getting warmed up. He placed sixth in his first Summer X Games. This surprised everyone because his opponents were the cream of the crop. They had concentrated on skateboarding throughout their careers, while White had just started skateboarding professionally. The performance clinched an ESPY Award from cable sports network ESPN for Best Action Sports Athlete of the Year—not bad for a high school sophomore!

Still, many people didn't realize that White had now been an extreme sports competitor for ten years. He had become accustomed to juggling snowboarding and skateboarding along with his personal life and schoolwork. White was competing in countries such as Japan, Chile, and Norway. But he was still just sixteen years old.

24

SHAUN WHITE FUN FACTS

• Shaun White is a talented ping-pong player. He owns a ping-pong table and has been known to wipe out those who dare to play against him.

• "Future Boy" and "The Flying Tomato" aren't the only nicknames White has had. He also has been called "The Egg" because of how he looks with a helmet on and "Señor Blanco," which means "Mister White" in Spanish. He has not really liked any of his nicknames.

• White is friends with talented figure skater Sasha Cohen, who was also a member of the 2006 U.S. Winter Olympic Team.

• One of White's favorite activities outside the world of extreme sports is playing the electric guitar. He spends much of his free time practicing.

▶ *Shaun White arrives at the 2003 ESPY Awards.*

▲ *Shaun White practices before a skateboarding competition in 2007.*

It wasn't easy. Part of him wanted to settle down and live a normal teenage life. But he knew that was impossible. And his competitive side would never have allowed it. He still had goals in both pro snowboarding and pro skateboarding that he wanted to accomplish. Every time he rode a snowboard or skateboard in an event, his desire to win overcame all other thoughts.

Meanwhile, the ties to his family and friends remained strong. Even after he had achieved great success in two sports, he found time to surf with his father and skate with his friends on the block. At home, his parents treated him like a normal teenager, not a superstar. He still had to clean his room, and he got in trouble for not following the house rules.

IN THE SPOTLIGHT

There was no mistaking that he had become famous worldwide. On one occasion in Japan he wore a red bandanna over his nose to shield it from the sun. Soon kids in Tokyo could be seen wearing red bandannas as well.

White was a natural with the media. He had always been easygoing, but he was never shy. He didn't go out of his way to promote himself and has never been self-centered. But he understood that the world was naturally curious about a kid with wild red hair who was on his way to dominating two sports. After all, how many athletes could claim that?

People began to wonder just how White made it all look so easy. Other athletes concentrated on their routines. But Shaun appeared carefree as he leaped five feet higher and mastered difficult twists and turns. He proved his claim that he performed better

▶ *When he's not competing, Shaun White is easygoing and laid-back.*

27

under greater pressure. And the more pressure that was on Shaun, the more relaxed he looked.

INJURY STRIKES

It seemed only an injury could slow him down—and it did in 2004. At seventeen years old, White was expecting to dominate the Winter X Games again. And he did in the early events. He took the gold medal in the slopestyle and finished the qualifying round of the superpipe with the top score. But after completing that run, he felt a sharp pain in his knee.

The injury turned out to be serious. White needed to undergo knee surgery in the spring. He was determined to come back, but he had little experience with knee injuries. He ended up returning to competition sooner than he should have. White quickly hurt the knee again and couldn't compete for another six months. For the first time in his career, he began to feel sorry for himself.

White's fellow snowboarders and skateboarders might not have felt too sorry for him. Without him dominating those sports, they knew they had a much better chance of winning. But their comfort level didn't stay high for very long. Shaun White returned in 2005. And he returned on top of his game.

The Unstoppable Star

White was one busy teenager in 2005. He not only competed on both the snowboarding and skateboarding tours full-time, but his income also continued to skyrocket. He was earning millions of dollars a year in endorsements.

▲ *Shaun White competes in the superpipe finals at the Winter X Games in 2005.*

SNOWBOARDING VERSUS SKATEBOARDING

Both sports use boards and can involve doing tricks in the air. So how are skateboarding and snowboarding different?

While some of the tricks are similar, snowboarders are strapped or locked onto their snowboard. Skateboarders aren't strapped on, and sometimes a skateboarder's feet will actually leave the board during a trick.

Skateboards and snowboards also move in different ways. Obviously, one slides, while the other rolls. Both skateboarders and snowboarders shift their weight when they change directions. Snowboarders also turn by digging the edges of their board into the snow. Since skateboarders can't dig into the pavement, they depend more on shifting their weight to control their motion.

While many people enjoy both snowboarding and skateboarding, few people excel at both to the extent that Shaun White has.

But could he win consistently in two sports? That was the question heading into 2005. White began his quest by winning the gold medal in slopestyle at the 2005 Winter X Games for the third straight year. And that same year, he won the skateboarding vert event for the Dew Action Sports Tour. White followed that up by placing second in the same event at the Summer X Games.

Though the best skateboarders in the world knew that he had potential for greatness in their sport, few believed he could establish himself as one of the best that quickly. But White understood that with the 2006 Winter Olympics coming up, he still needed to concentrate on snowboarding. He even traveled to New Zealand in the summer of 2005 to take advantage of the country's cold, snowy weather.

ALL THE RIGHT MOVES

While training for the Winter Olympics, White continued to perfect moves his fellow snowboarders simply couldn't perform. He showed an unusual talent in the half-pipe. Most riders were able to muster one 1080 (three turns around) in their routines. But Shaun amazed everyone by sandwiching two 1080s between two 900-degree spins. His ability to

▼ *Shaun White flies through the air at the U.S. Snowboard Grand Prix in 2006.*

▲ *Shaun White* (left) *and teammate Daniel Kass celebrate their Olympic medals.*

make such moves placed him above all other half-pipe riders. "Going into a 1080 with a 900—no one else has been able to do that," said U.S. half-pipe coach Bud Keene heading into the 2006 Winter Olympics. "Shaun is head and shoulders above the rest. He's clearly the guy to beat."

White showed his talent in the qualifying events for the Winter Olympics. But that was merely a warm-up to the most remarkable string of performances of his career. Shaun won the Olympic gold medal. But he also took first place in the half-pipe in events in Vermont, New Jersey, Oregon, and Colorado. He won gold medals in the slopestyle in Vermont and Colorado. In fact, he won nearly all of the snowboarding contests he entered in 2006. He was in a league of his own.

STILL GOING STRONG

White didn't slow down a bit after winning his Olympic gold medal. But his newfound fame also required his attention. Winning the Winter X Games certainly made him well known to fans of extreme sports. But the Olympic gold medal also brought White into the spotlight among mainstream sports fans and older generations. Just about everyone knew who he was. What he achieved at the Olympics increased his popularity and media attention even more.

Rolling Stone magazine featured White on its cover a month after the Winter Games. He became the first snowboarder to grace the cover of *Sports Illustrated*. He also appeared on *The Tonight Show with Jay Leno*, the most-watched late-night program in the United States. People who had never followed extreme sports were taking note when White won two Winter X Games gold medals and five U.S. Snowboarding Grand Prix championships in 2006—not to mention his Olympic gold medal.

▶ *Shaun White, pictured in 2006, has reached celebrity status.*

33

A MEMORABLE TRIP

Shaun White has traveled all over the world. One of his most memorable visits was to the African nation of Rwanda in 2007. The country had been devastated by a war in which many people were killed.

White went to Rwanda with a group called Right to Play, which works with children in third-world countries. The organization uses play and sports to teach life skills. During White's visit to Rwanda, he spent time with orphans whose parents had been killed in the war. He gave the orphan children skateboards and put on a skateboarding display for them.

White said he wasn't trying to get the children involved in skateboarding. He was just trying to take their minds off their troubles. He admitted that the visit to Rwanda was emotionally tough for him.

White had become one of the wealthiest teenagers in the country. By 2007, he was earning an estimated $6 million a year in winnings and endorsements. He helped create a snowboarding DVD titled *The White Album*. He appeared in a documentary titled *The First Descent*. And, he signed a contract to help create a video snowboarding game.

"There will never be another Shaun White," said snowboarder Jack Ridenour. "He's like [basketball star] Michael Jordan or [Super Bowl quarterback] John Elway—there's only one."

White competes on the superpipe at the 2008 Winter X Games. ▶
He placed first in the competition.

Conquering Two Sports

White admitted that the explosion of media attention and endorsement deals took away from his performance in late 2006 and early 2007. He still hadn't reached his potential in skateboarding. And he even began struggling in snowboarding. He earned just a silver medal in the superpipe event and a bronze in the slopestyle event at the 2007 Winter X Games. Finally, he recovered to win the gold medal in the half-pipe event at the U.S. Open.

White felt that he simply didn't have enough time to practice properly. "I'd been doing all those photo shoots, TV, interviews, and then I'd be like, 'Okay, I *need* this week to practice,'" White said. "Then out of nowhere someone would call up to do something really amazing, and I was like, 'I gotta do it.'"

Fame was taking up his time even outside the world of television and newspapers. After winning an Olympic gold medal, White attended the Los Angeles premiere of Al Gore's documentary on global warming, *An Inconvenient Truth*.

◄ *Shaun White continues to dazzle extreme sports fans with his skills and tricks.*

BECOMING A HOMEOWNER

When Shaun White was moving into his new home north of San Diego, his neighbors watched with curiosity. They saw what looked to be a teenage boy (he was twenty at the time) and assumed it couldn't have been his own house.

"The neighbors," White remembers, "were like, 'We were watching you and wondering when the parents were going to show up.'"

Of course, the neighbors were wrong. White had purchased the home with the money he earned in endorsements and as an extreme sports champion.

He snowboarded with talk show host Montel Williams and appeared in ads for some of the biggest companies in America. In 2008, Target stores started carrying a Shaun White clothing line. Not to mention, girls he didn't even know started inviting him to their high school proms. They scribbled their invitations with chalk on the driveway of his Carlsbad home.

White expected attention after taking the gold. But this was far more than he anticipated. "It's getting a little crazy," he said. "I think that's been the biggest surprise. I knew it was going to be huge, and I knew that I would get a lot of opportunities from that and a lot of success. But, I don't know, not to the degree that it's still going on."

▲ *White has been overwhelmed with attention since winning an Olympic gold medal.*

Meanwhile, White was taking on more responsibility in his personal life. He had earned so much money by age sixteen that he was able to buy the Carlsbad home in which he still lived. That way, his parents no longer had to make payments on it.

Four years later he bought his own home just north of San Diego. It has a huge outdoor TV screen and a pool that turns into a waterfall at the edge of a cliff.

▲ *Shaun White waves to the crowd after a win in 2007.*

White spends time there when he isn't traveling for competitions.

The time away from home began paying off after the 2007 Winter X Games. First, White dominated the snowboarding world again. He won all six half-pipe events he entered after the X Games. And he finished in the top three in every slopestyle competition as well. White also was competing more successfully in skateboarding. He won three consecutive vert events in 2007.

But the Flying Tomato was saving his most breathtaking extreme sports performance for the Winter X Games in 2008. He achieved for the first time what few other snowboarders could even consider attempting. That day, strong winds were making landings difficult, and a heavy snowstorm limited visibility in the superpipe. Still, Shaun White nailed a 1260—three-and-a-half spins—and a perfect landing.

ACHIEVEMENTS

Shaun White has won many competitions over the years. Here is a sampling of what the young snowboarder and skateboarder has accomplished:

2008
- Won U.S. Open superpipe and slopestyle
- Won Winter X Games superpipe

2007
- Won AST Skate Vert Championship
- Named *Transworld Snowboarding* Rider of the Year and one of *Snowboarding Magazine*'s Top Ten Riders of the Year

2006
- Won Winter Olympics half-pipe gold medal
- Won Winter X Games half-pipe and slopestyle
- Won U.S. Open half-pipe and slopestyle

2005
- Won Chevy Grand Prix Olympic Qualifier #1 and #2
- Won Honda Session-at-Vail slopestyle and rail jam
- Won FIS World Cup Lake Placid

2004
- Won Innsbruck Air and Style
- Won Winter X Games slopestyle

2003
- Won Winter X Games half-pipe and slopestyle
- Won Bear Mountain Vans Triple Crown half-pipe and slopestyle
- Won Phillips U.S. Open slopestyle

The crowd in Aspen, Colorado, roared with delight and amazement.

"I was going at that wall and just wanted to spin as hard as I could," White said. "Pretty much riding away from that [1260] was the best feeling ever."

White nailed consecutive 1080s in the opening round. Then, he did the same in the next round before almost achieving the 1260. And in the finals, he was nearly perfect, capping his run with the 1260 to win the superpipe gold with ease.

It was clear that White was still the best snowboarder in the world. But he was quick to point out that if skateboarding was accepted as a sport in the Summer Olympics, he might just take the winter off to practice it. That way, he could be the first athlete ever to win a gold medal in both the winter and summer games.

"It would definitely be one of the craziest things I've ever done," White said. "It would elevate my skating to another level because I'd never had that much time. It would have to be the point with snowboarding where I've done everything—which is getting pretty close. You have to be motivated to do something new. It's getting harder these days."

Shaun White raises his snowboard after yet another victory ▶
at the 2007 Winter X Games.

Timeline

1986 Shaun White is born in Carlsbad, California, on September 3

1992 Learns to ride a snowboard

1993 Wins the first snowboard competition he enters

2000 Becomes a professional snowboarder after accepting an endorsement deal

2001 Achieves first top-ten finish in both slopestyle and superpipe at the Winter X Games

2002 Wins silver medals in both events at the Winter X Games

2003 Becomes youngest slopestyle champion in Winter X Games history; competes in skateboarding at the Summer X Games

2004 Wins first in the Winter X Games slopestyle event

2005 Becomes first athlete to win medals in both Winter and Summer X Games

2006 Earns gold medal in the half-pipe at Winter Olympics in Italy

2007 Wins the skateboarding vert in three straight events; wins the half-pipe at the U.S. Open

2008 Achieves near-impossible 1260 spin and wins superpipe at the Winter X Games

Further Info

Books

Doeden, Matt. *Shaun White*. Minneapolis: Lerner Publications Company, 2007.

Young, Jeff. *Shaun White*. Greensboro, NC: Morgan Reynolds Publishing, 2008.

CDs and DVDs

Shaun White: Don't Look Down. ESPN, 2008.

The White Album. Cinemaseaone, 2004.

Internet Addresses

Official Shaun White Web site
http://www.shaunwhite.com

Snowboarder magazine rider profile
http://www.snowboardermag.com/features/riderprofiles/shaun-white-07

Glossary

Backside 900—A snowboarding move that involves two-and-a-half clockwise spins in the air.

endorsement—Deal in which an athlete earns money to promote a product.

extreme sports—Fast-paced sports outside the mainstream, such as snowboarding and skateboarding.

Frontside 1080—A snowboarding move that involves three full counterclockwise spins in the air.

gold medal—The first-place prize in any Olympic or X Games sport.

McTwist—A trick that requires one-and-a-half spins while doing a front flip.

Olympics—A competition in summer and winter sports for athletes from all over the world.

vert—A skateboarding event that is held on a U-shaped vertical ramp.

X Games—Extreme sports competitions that take place annually in both the summer and winter.

Index